NORSK FOLKEMUSEUM

Copyright: A/S Chr. Olsen-Mittet, Norsk Folkemuseum
and the curators and staff of the Educational Department
of the Museum.
Printed and bound 1987 by KINA Italia SpA, Milan
Photographs by Jac. Brun and the Norwegian Folk Museum's
own photographers: Bjørg Disington, Anne-Lise Schiødt and
Bergljot Sinding.
Layout: Jac. Brun
Photosetting: Kreativ Sats A/S, Norway
ISBN 82-7182-082-6 hf

1. Inngang
   Main Entrance
2. Torget
   Marketplace
3. Teateret
   Theatre
4. Festplassen
   The Green
5. Pottemakeri
   Pottery
6. Farmasihistorisk Museum
   Pharmacological Museum
7. Sølvsmedverksted
   Silversmith's Workshop
8. Restaürant
   Restaurant
9. Kafé
   Café

Omslagets forside: Loft og bur fra Rofshus, Mo i Telemark, bygget i 1754.

Front cover: Storehouses from Rofshus, Mo, Telemark (1754).

Titelseite: Vorratshäuser aus Rofshus, Mo in Telemark, errichtet 1754.

Sur la couverture, devant: Maisonnette à étage et cellier, érigés en 1754 et provenant de Mo, dans le Telemark.

Norsk Folkemuseum, Norges største kulturhistoriske museum, ble startet i 1894 av den da knapt 25 år gamle Hans Aall.

Norsk Folkemuseum er et riksmuseum, og har derfor til oppgave å vise hvordan mennesker, fattige og rike, i by og land, har levet og arbeidet i Norge fra reformasjonen (1500-tallet) og frem til i dag.

Friluftsmuseet som er landets eldste, dekker et areal på ca. 140 mål, og består av omkring 140 gamle hus hentet fra de forskjellige deler av landet. Hus fra bygdene er samlet i tun, karakteristiske for de enkelte distrikter, mens byhusene er samlet i museets «Gamleby».

Blant mengden av hus finnes også flere bygninger fra middelalderen, bl.a. Gol Stavkirke fra omkring 1200 og Raulandstua, et av de eldste bolighus av tre vi kjenner til i Norge. I sommersesongen holdes katolsk messe eller evangelisk luthersk gudstjeneste i stavkirken hver søndag.

I de innendørs samlinger, som omfatter mer enn 180.000 gjenstander, finnes møbler og annet husgeråd, rosemaling og treskurd, drakter og vevnader til nytte og pryd. Redskaper fra jord- og skogbruk illustrerer gamle tradisjonelle driftsformer.

En utstilling av ride- og kjøretøy forteller om transportmidler i et land som lenge var uegnet for kjøretøy med hjul.

Det finnes en Musikksamling og en Kirkesamling hvor det også gis konserter på museets egne instrumenter. Samisk avdeling belyser samenes gamle kultur med jakt, fiske og reindrift, foruten både kvinnelig og mannlig husflid.

Museet har restaurant med peisestuer og friluftsservering og sentralt beliggende kafé for enklere servering. På søndager i sommersesongen og enkelte aftener opptrer folkedansgrupper i museet. Museet har også en egen dansegruppe.

The Norwegian Folk Museum, Norway's largest museum of cultural history, was founded in 1894 by Hans Aall. Aall, who was barely twenty-five years old at the time, was later appointed its first director.

The Museum is a national institution, and accordingly aims to show how the people of Norway, from town and country, rich and poor alike, have lived and worked from the Reformation (16th century) to the present day.

The open-air section, the oldest collection of its kind in the country, is 140,000 square metres (3,500 acres) in extent and comprises some 140 old buildings, transported to the site from all over Norway. The rural dwellings are grouped together by region of origin, while the urban houses have been laid out to form an «Old Town». The collection includes a number of buildings from the Middle Ages, among them Gol stave church (c. 1200) and Raulandstua, one of the oldest wooden dwellings extant in Norway. In summer a Roman Catholic mass or an Evangelical Lutheran service is held in the church on Sundays.

The indoor section, which comprises more than 180,000 exhibits, contains furniture, household fittings and utensils, examples of the «rose-painter's» and wood-carver's art, clothing, and tapestries and other woven work for decoration and everyday use. Farming implements and logging gear illustrate the development of the agricultural and forestry industries, and a collection of riding gear, trappings and conveyances provides an interesting picture of the history of transportation in a country whose roads for long defied wheeled vehicles.

There are also music and ecclesiastical sections, in which recitals are held on the Museum's own instruments.

The Lapp section provides a fascinating insight into the ancient culture of this ethnic group, a culture which was based on hunting, fishing and reindeer herding, and it also houses examples of Lapp art and handicrafts, the work of both men and women.

The museum boasts a restaurant and a centrally located café where lighter meals and refreshments are served. On Sundays and selected evenings in summer displays of folk-dancing are staged by visiting troupes, as well as by the Museum's own dancers.

Telemarkstunet
The Telemark farmstead.
Der Binnenhof Telemark.
Le groupe des maisons du Telemark.

Das Norwegische Volksmuseum, das grösste kulturhistorische Museum Norwegens, wurde 1894 von dem damals kaum 25-jährigen Hans Aall gegründet.

Das Norwegische Volksmuseum ist ein Reichsmuseum. Seine Aufgabe ist daher zu veranschaulichen, wie die Menschen, arm und reich, in der Stadt und auf dem Lande, von der Reformation an (um 1500) und bis auf unsere Tage in Norwegen gelebt und gearbeitet haben.

Das Freiluftmuseum, das älteste des Landes, deckt eine Fläche von etwa 140 Da, und besteht aus etwa 140 alten Häusern, die aus verschiedenen Landesteilen geholt wurden. Die Häuser von den Ortschaften sind in Binnenhöfe, charakteristisch für die jeweiligen Bezirke, gesammelt, während die Stadthäuser in der «Altstadt» des Museums gesammelt sind.

Unter der grossen Anzahl der Häuser sind auch mehrere Gebäude aus dem Mittelalter, u.a. Gol Stabkirche, etwa um 1200 erbaut, und die Raulandkate, eins der ältesten Wohnhäuser aus Holz, die heute in Norwegen bekannt sind.

In der Sommersaison wird sonntags in der Stabkirche katholische Messe oder evangelisch/lutherschen Gottesdienst gehalten. In den Sammlungen der Innenräume, die mehr als 180.000 Gegenstände umfassen, gehören Möbel und sonstige Hausgeräte, Rosenmalerei und Holzschnitzkunst, sowie Trachten und Gewebe zu Nutzen und Zierde. Alte Geräte von Land- und Waldwirtschaft gewähren einen Einblick in die traditionellen Betriebsformen.

Die Ausstellung der Reitgeschirre und Fahrzeuge berichtet über Verkehrsmittel in einem Lande, in dem der Gebrauch von Fahrzeugen mit Rädern lange unmöglich war.

Dazu gibt es noch eine Musiksammlung und eine Kirchensammlung. Hier werden mitunter Konzerte mit den Museumsinstrumenten gegeben.

Die Lappische Abteilung erläutet die Kultur der Lappen, ihre Jagd, ihren Fischfang und Renntierbetrieb, sowie die männliche und weibliche Handarbeit.

Das Museum hat ein Restaurant mit Kaminzimmern, ein Terrassencafé sowie ein zentral gelegenes Imbisslokal.

Sonntags in der Sommersaison, mitunter auch abends an Werktagen, werden Volkstanzvorführungen im Museum gegeben. Das Museum verfügt über eine eigene Tanzgruppe.

Norsk Folkemuseum, — Musée National Folklorique de Norvège —, le plus grand des musées norvégiens dans le domaine de l'histoire de la civilisation, fut fondé en 1894 par Hans Aall, qui alors n'était âgé que de 25 ans. Musée national, il a pour tâche de montrer comment, depuis la Réforme (XVIème siècle) et jusqu'à nos jours, les gens — riches et pauvres — ont vécu et travaillé en Norvège.

S'étendant sur quelque 14 hectares, le musée de plein air, le plus vieux du pays, comprend environ 140 vieilles maisons provenant des diverses provinces de celui-ci. Les maisons ramenées de localités campagnardes sont disposées de manière à former des cours, chacune caractéristique de telle ou telle région, tandis que les maisons urbaines sont réunies dans la «Vieille Ville». Parmi toutes ces maisons, on remarque aussi quelques constructions datant du Moyen-Age, entre autres l'église en bois debout de Gol, édifice qui date des alentours de 1200, et le séjour de Rauland, une des plus vieilles demeures en bois conservées en Norvège. Chaque dimanche tout au long de la saison d'été, on célèbre tour à tour une messe catholique ou un office luthérien dans cette église en bois.

Composées de plus de 130.000 objets, les collections renfermées dans les maisons comprennent des meubles et des ustensiles de ménage divers, des pièces à décoration florale peinte et des oeuvres en taille de bois, des costumes et de vieilles tapisseries utilitaires et décoratives. Ustensiles agraires et ustensiles forestiers nous renseignent sur les modes d'exploitation traditionnels d'autrefois.

Une exposition permanente de sellerie et de véhicules nous relate l'histoire des moyens de transport dans un pays dont le terrain est longtemps resté peu carrossable.

Il y a encore un musée du culte et une collection musicologique où l'on donne des concerts d'instruments appartenant au musée même.

La section laponne nous documente sur la vieille civilisation des Lapons, basée sur la chasse, la pêche et l'exploitation des rennes, et nous fait voir des réalisations artisanales domestiques, de femmes et d'hommes.

Le musée a un restaurant aménagé dans des salles chauffées au feu ouvert, un buffet de plein air, ainsi qu'un café, situé au centre, pour des collations légères.

Pendant la saison d'été, il y a, tous les dimanches et parfois encore en semaine, alors en soirée, des présentations de groupes de danses folkloriques. Le musée a par ailleurs son propre groupe de danseurs.

Øverst: Loft og bur står ofte sammen i Telemark. Tveitoloftet fra omkring år 1300, var gårdens gjestehus og «skattkammer». Vengjeburet fra Nedre Nisi, reist i 1797, var et forrådshus. Betegnelsen «vengjebur» viser til svalene på sidene.
Til venstre: Kvinnebunad fra Vest-Telemark.

Top: One- and two-storey storehouses were often placed side by side in Telemark. This two-storey building, Tveitoloftet (c. 1300), served both as a storehouse and to house guests. The other building, a «vengjebur», erected in 1797, was used only as a storehouse.
Left: "Bunad" from western Telemark.

Oben: In Telemark stehen Die ein—und zweistöckigen Vorratshäuser und Gästehaus oft zusammen. Das Vorratshaus von Tveito, etwa um 1300, war sogleich Gästehaus und «Schatzkammer» des Hofes. «Vengjeburet» von Nedre Nisi, errichtet 1797, war ein Vorratshaus. Die Bezeichnung «Vengjebur» bezieht sich auf die Umgänge mit Vordach (svaler).
Links: Frauentracht aus West-Telemark.

En haut: Dans le Telemark, la maisonnette à étage et le cellier se trouvent souvent groupés ensemble. A Tveito, la maisonnette à étage, datant des alentours de l'an 1300, servait de «trésor» et de séjour d'amis. Le cellier «à ailes» de Nedre Nisi, construit en 1797, était une chambre de réserves. L'épithète «à ailes» fait allusion aux galeries qui le flanquent.
A gauche: Costume de femme provenant du Telemark occidental.

Øverst: Loftet fra Grimsgard, Nes i Hallingdal, er fra ca. 1700, men svalen er datert 1797. Sammenligning med Tveitoloftet viser hvordan denne bygningstypen holdt seg nesten uendret gjennom 500 år.
Til venstre: Skolebarn på besøk i Hallingdalstunet.

Top: This storehouse from Grimsgard Farm, Nes, Hallingdal, dates from about 1700, but the gallery is of later origin (1797). A comparison with Tveitoloftet reveals how the architectural style remained virtually unchanged over five centuries.
Left: Schoolchildren visiting the Hallingdal farmstead.

Oben: Vorratshaus von Grimsgard, Nes in Hallingdal, etwa 1700 errichtet; das Vordach ist jedoch 1797 datiert. Ein Vergleich mit dem Vorratshaus Tveito zeigt, dass dieser Baustil durch fast 500 Jahre ungeändert geblieben ist.
Links: Schulkinder besuchen den Binnenhof Hallingdal.

En haut: La maisonnette à étage de Grimsgard (Nes, dans la Hallingdal) date d'environ 1700, mais la galerie de la façade porte toutefois la date de 1797. Son rapprochement d'avec la maisonnette de Tveito nous prouve que ce mode de construction est resté presque invariable pendant 500 ans.
A gauche: Des écoliers visitant le groupe de maisons de la Hallingdal.

Øverst: Numedalstunet med stua fra Væråsmo som nummer to fra venstre, og Raulandstua helt til høyre.
Til høyre: Interiør i Væråsmostua fra Flesberg. Stua ble bygget i slutten av 1700-årene.

Top: The Numedal farmstead. The cabin («stua») second from the left is from Væråsmo, Flesberg, and that on the far right, Raulandstua, from Uvdal.
Right: Interior of the Væråsmo cabin (late 18th century).

Oben: Der Binnenhof Numedal. Die Kate aus Væråsmo ist Nr. 2 von links. Ganz rechts die Raulandskate.
Rechts: Interieur der Væråsmokate aus Flesberg, erbaut Ende 1700.

En haut: La cour formée par les maisons provenant de la Numedal, avec le séjour de Væråsmo en deuxième position à compter de la gauche, et avec le séjour de Rauland tout à fait sur la droite.
A droite: L'intérieur du séjour de Væråsmo, de Flesberg, construit vers la fin du XVIIIème siècle.

Øverst: Inngangspartiet på Raulandstua fra Uvdal.
Til venstre: Raulandstua, bygget ca. 1300, er blant de eldste bevarte bolighus i Norge.

Top: Doorway of the Rauland cabin.
Left: Raulandstua (c. 1300), one of the oldest dwelling-houses extant in Norway.

Oben: Eingangspartie der Raulandskate aus Uvdal.
Links: Das Wohnhaus aus Rauland, Uvdal, etwa 1300, ist eins der ältesten bewahrten Wohnhäuser in Norwegen.

En haut: L'entrée du séjour de Rauland, de l'Uvdal.
A gauche: Le séjour de Rauland qui, construit aux alentours de l'an 1300, est une des plus vieilles maisons d'habitation de Norvège.

Til høyre: Kvinnebunad fra Setesdal.
Nederst: Tunet fra Setesdal er anlagt med innhusene på rekke øverst og en uthusrekke nederst i terrenget, slik skikken var i Setesdal.

Right: "Bunad" from Setesdal.
Bottom: To accord with local custom this Setesdal farmstead has its main buildings set in a row higher up and the outhouses in another row lower down.

Rechts: Frauentracht aus Setesdal.
Unten: Der Binnenhof aus Setesdal wurde gemäss der örtlichen Gebräuche im Gelände so angelegt, dass die Wohnhäuser in der oberen Reihe und die Wirtschaftsgebäude in der unteren Reihe liegen.

A droite: Costume de femme, provenant de la Setesdal.
En bas: Dans la cour formée par les maisons de Setesdal, les maisons d'habitation se succèdent dans la partie haute du terrain, tandis que les dépendances se trouvent en contrebas, conformément à l'usage dans cette contrée.

Stua fra Åmlid er 300 år gammel, men innredningen følger skikkene fra middelalderen. Slik bodde folk i Setesdal til langt inn i 1800-årene, lenge etter at østlendingene fikk peis og vinduer.

Although this cabin from Åmlid is only 300 years old, its layout and furnishings adhere to the mediaeval pattern. The inhabitants of the Setesdal valley lived thus till well into the 19th century, long after their east-Norwegian countrymen had adopted fireplaces with chimneys and windows.

Das Wohnhaus aus Åmlid ist 300 Jahre alt, die Einrichtung entspricht jedoch den Gebräuchen des Mittelalters. So wohnten Leute in Setesdal bis ins 19. Jahrhundert und noch lange nachdem in Südost-Norwegen Kamine und Fenster eingeführt waren.

Bien que le séjour d'Åmlid n'ait que 300 ans, son aménagement prolonge les traditions médiévales. Tel fut le logement des habitants de la Setesdal, bien avant dans le XIXème siècle, et longtemps après que ceux de la province d'Østlandet eurent équipé leurs demeures de fenêtres et d'âtres à cheminée.

Øverst: Østerdalstunet sett fra vest. Barfrø-stua fra Trønnes i Stor-Elvdal, 1670, til venstre i bildet.
Nederst: Interiør fra barfrøstua med innredning fra 1808.

Top: The Østerdal farmstead from the west. On the left is "Barfrøstua", a cabin from Trønnes, Stor-Elvdal (1670).
Bottom: Interior of the "Barfrø" cabin, with furnishings from 1808. A "barfrø" is a two-storey porch.

Oben: Binnenhof aus Østerdalen, vom Westen gesehen. Links im Bild ein Wohnhaus namens «Barfrøstua» aus Trønnes, Stor-Elvdal, 1670.
Unten: Interieur des Barfrø-Hauses. Einrichtung aus dem Jahre 1808.

En haut: La cour formée par les maisons provenant de la province d'Østerdal, côté ouest. Dans la partie gauche, la maison dite du «Barfrø» (= à «étage-tourelle»), de Trønnes dans la Stor-Elvdal (1670).
En bas: Vue intérieure de la maison du «Barfrø», dont l'aménagement date de 1808.

Øverst på begge sider: Seter fra Gudbrandsdalen.
Motstående side, nederst: Saueklipping foregår på museet hver høst en søndag i september.
Til høyre: Kvinne- og mannsbunad fra Gudbrandsdalen.

Top spread: A Gudbrandsdal summer outfarm («seter»).
Facing page, bottom: Sheepshearing takes place annually on a Sunday in September.
Right: "Bunads" (a man's and woman's) from Gudbrandsdal.

Oben auf beiden Seiten: Alm aus Gudbrandsdal.
Gegenüberliegende Seite, unten: An einem Sonntag im September werden die Schafe geschoren.
Rechts: Frauentracht und Männertracht aus Gudbrandsdal.

En haut, à cheval sur les deux pages: Chalet de la Gudbrandsdal.
Ci-contre; en bas: Tous les ans, à l'automne, un dimanche de septembre, c'est la tonte des moutons du Musée.
A droite: Costumes masculin et féminin provenant de la Gudbrandsdal.

15

«Kong Oscar II's samlinger» er verdens eldste friluftsmuseum, grunnlagt i 1881. De fem husene i kongens private samling ble overtatt av Norsk Folkemuseum i 1907.

Side 16 og 17: Stavkirken fra Gol i Hallingdal er fra omkring år 1200. Mye av eksteriøret er rekonstruert, men det meste av interiøret og hovedkonstruksjonen er opprinnelig. «Stavene» er de bærende søylene som sammen med svillene danner rammer for stående veggplanker. De frittstående «stavene» inne i kirken bærer taket. De malte dekorasjonene i kor og apsis er fra 1652.

Til venstre: Portalen med sammenslyngede drager i treskurd.

Founded in 1881, King Oscar II's collection constitutes the world's oldest open-air museum. The five buildings in the King's private collection passed to the Norwegian Folk Museum in 1907.

Pages 16 and 17: The stave church from Gol, Hallingdal, dates from c. 1200. Much of the exterior has been restored, but most of the interior and the principal structural features are original. The «staves» are the supporting uprights, which, together with the sills, form the framework for the vertical wall-planks. The freestanding «staves» inside the church support the roof. The painted decorations in the choir and apse date from 1652.

Left: The entrance, with its elabaorately carved intertwined dragons.

Die Sammlungen des Königs Oscar II, die älteste museale Freiluftanlagen der Welt, wurden 1881 gegründet. Die fünf Häuser der Privatsammlung des Königs wurden 1907 vom Norwegischen Volksmuseum übernommen.

Seite 16 und 17: Die Stabkirche aus Gol in Hallingdal wurde etwa um 1200 errichtet. Ein betrachtlicher Teil des Exterieurs ist rekonstruiert; weitgehend ursprünglich sind jedoch die Inneneinrichtungen und die Hauptkonstruktionen. Die «Stäbe» sind Tragbalken, welche zusammen mit den Schwellbalken die Rahmen der stehenden Wandbretter bilden. Die freistehenden «Stäbe» in der Kirche tragen das Dach. Die gemalten Dekorationen im Chor und in der Apsis sind aus dem Jahre 1652.

Links: Die Holzschnitzerei des Portals stellt zusammengeflochtene Drachen dar.

Les collections du Roi Oscar II constituent le plus vieux musée de plein air du monde (fondé en 1881). Les cinq maisons de la collection privée du Roi furent remises au Musée National Folklorique en 1907.

Pages 16 et 17: L'église en bois debout provenant de Gol dans la Hallingdal date des alentours de 1200. Si son extérieur a en grande partie été reconstruit, la majeure partie de l'intérieur, ainsi que le corps principal, sont d'origine. Les «bois debout», ce sont les poteaux porteurs qui, conjointement avec les solives, forment les chassis des planches verticales des parois. Les poteaux de la nef portent la toiture. Les décorations peintes du coeur et de l'abside datent de 1652.

A gauche: Le portail, décoré de dragons entrelacés en taille de bois.

Hovestua fra Heddal i Telemark var det første huset i «Oscar II's samlinger». Det ble bygget i 1738, og stod på en velstandsgård. Innredningen er som i en vanlig bondestue med peis.

Hovestua from Heddal, Telemark, was the first building in Oscar II's collection. Built in 1738, it was part of a prosperous farm. It is furnished like a regular farmhouse, and has a fireplace with chimney.

Das Hove-Haus aus Heddal in Telemark war das erste Haus in den «Sammlungen des Königs Oscar II». Es wurde 1738 auf einem wohlhabenden Bauernhof gebaut. Die Einrichtung entspricht jedoch der einer üblichen Kate mit offenem Kamin.

La maison d'apparat de Heddal, dans le Telemark, fut la première à entrer dans la collection d'Oscar II. Construite en 1738, elle se trouvait initialement à une propriété de paysan fortuné. Son aménagement correspond à ce qui était habituel pour la maison de paysan, avec âtre à cheminée.

Berdalsloftet fra 1750-årene kommer fra Nesland i Telemark. Det har rike utskjæringer og sval på alle fire sidene.

This storehouse, Berdalsloftet, is from Nesland, Telemark, and dates from the 1750s. Richly carved, it has a gallery on all four sides.

Das Vorratshaus «Berdal», etwa 1750, stammt aus Nesland in Telemark. Es ist mit reichen Schnitzereien versehen und hat an allen vier Seiten Umgang mit Vordach.

La maisonnette à étage de Berdal date des années 1750 et provient de Nesland, dans le Telemark. Richement décorée en taille de bois, elle est équipée de galeries formant un pourtour complet.

Soveloftet fra Rolstad i Sør-Fron er fra slutten av 1200-årene. Det står rett på bakken slik som alle loft gjorde i middelalderen.

Dating from the late 13th century, this building, used primarily as sleeping quarters, is from Rolstad, Sør-Fron. Like mediaeval storehouses, it rests directly on the ground.

Schlafhaus (soveloft) aus Rolstad in Sør-Fron, Ende 1200. Es ist direkt auf der Erde ohne Fundamente angelegt, entsprechend der im Mittelalter üblichen Bauweise dieser Häuser.

La maisonnette dortoir de Rolstad, dans le Sør-Fron, date de la fin du XIIIème siècle. Elle se trouve plantée directement sur le terrain, comme le furent d'ailleurs toutes les maisonnettes à étage du Moyen-Age.

Husene på husmannsplassen kommer fra Trøndelag.
Øverst: Til høyre i bildet, «uppstugu» fra Mjøen i Oppdal, med loft over forstue og kove.
Nederst: Interiør fra fjøset.

Cotters' cabins from Trøndelag.
Top: On the right of the picture is an «uppstugu» from Mjøen, Oppdal, with a loft above the entrance hall and bedroom.
Bottom: Interior of the byre.

Die Häuslerkaten stammen aus Trøndelag.
Oben, rechts im Bild: Wohnhaus aus Mjøen in Oppdal, mit Dachgeschoss über Vorstube und Alkoven.
Unten: Interieur vom Rinderstall.

Les maisons de la métairie nous viennent du Trøndelag.
En haut: La partie droite de la reproduction nous montre la «maison haute» de Mjøen, en Oppdal, avec grenier au-dessus d'un vestibule et d'une petite chambre.
En bas: Vue intérieure de l'étable.

Øverst: «Trønderlåna» fra Stiklestad i Verdal, oppført ca. 1795, er typisk for de langstrakte våningshusene i landsdelen.

Top: Built about 1795, «Trønderlåna» from Stiklestad, Verdal, is typical of the long farmhouses of this part of Norway.

Oben: Das Bauernhaus «Trønderlåna» aus Stiklestad in Verdal, errichtet etwa 1795, ist ein typisches Beispiel der langgestreckten Wohnhäuser dieses Landesteils.

En haut: Erigée aux alentours de 1795, la «Trønderlåna» (= la «maison allongée du Trøndelag»), de Stiklestad dans la Verdal, est un exemple typique des maisons d'habitation étirées de cette province.

Øverst, til venstre: Klyngetun fra Hardanger.
Til høyre: Fra eldhuset i tunet.
Nederst, til venstre: Kone- og jentebunad fra Hardanger.
Til høyre: Bryllupsbord i røykovnstua fra Nes på Varaldsøy.
Motstående side, nederst til venstre: Interiør fra sengebu, Ytre Sæle, Bygstad i Sunnfjord, 1684.
Til høyre: Kone i vinterdrakt fra Voss.

Top left: A farmstead from Hardanger.
Right: The «cookhouse».
Bottom, left: Married and unmarried women's «bunads» from Hardanger.
Right: A table laid for a wedding feast in a log cabin («røykovnstua») from Nes, Varaldsøy.
Facing page, bottom left: Sleeping quarters, Ytre Sæle, Bygstad, Sunnfjord (1684).
Right: A married woman in winter costume from Voss.

Oben links: Häusergruppe aus Hardanger.
Rechts: Interieur vom Feuerhaus des Binnenhofes.
Unten links: Frauentracht und Mädchentracht aus Hardanger.
Rechts: Hochzeitstisch in der Rauchofen-Stube aus Nes auf der Insel Varaldsøy.
Gegenüberliegende Seite, unten links: Interieur eines Schlafhauses, Ytre Sæle, Bygstad in Sunnfjord, 1684.
Rechts: Frau in Wintertracht aus Voss.

En haut et à gauche: Groupe serré de maisons, de Hardanger.
A droite: Vue intérieure de la hutte de chauffe.
En bas et à gauche: Costumes de Hardanger, de femme mariée d'une part, de jeune fille d'autre part.
A droite: Table de mariage, dressée dans la salle à âtre ouvert, de Nes à Varaldsøy.
Ci-contre, en bas et à gauche: Intérieur d'une hutte à dormir, d'Ytre Sæle, à Bygstad, dans la province de Sunnfjord (1684).
A droite: Femme en habit d'hiver, de Voss.

Øverst: Bunader fra Sogn.
Nederst: Prestegårdsbygning fra Leikanger i Sogn. Hagen foran huset er anlagt etter barokkens krav til symmetri og regularitet.
Motstående side, øverst: Innredningen i prestegården består av portretter og møbler etter familien Thaulow.

Top: «Bunads» from Sogn.
Bottom: Parsonage from Leikanger, Sogn. The garden is typically baroque in its symmetry.
Facing page, top: The present furnishings and portraits of the parsonage were once the property of the Thaulow family.

Oben: Trachten aus Sogn.
Unten: Das Pfarrhofgebäude aus Leikanger, Sogn. Der Garten vor dem Hause wurde entsprechend den Anforderungen des Barocks zur Symmetrie und Regularität angelegt.
Gegenüberliegende Seite, oben: Die Einrichtung des Pfarrhofes umfasst die Porträtsammlung und die Möbel nach der Familie Thaulow.

En haut: Costumes, de la province de Sogn.
En bas: La maison presbytérale de Leikanger. Le jardin devant la maison est aménagé conformément aux exigences du baroque pour ce qui est de la symétrie et de la régularité.
Ci-contre, en haut: L'ameublement de la maison presbytérale est constitué de meubles et de portraits ayant appartenu à la famille Thaulow.

Folkedans er et fast
innslag på museet
hele sommeren.

Folk-dancing dis-
plays are a regular
summer attraction.

Den ganzen Som-
mer hindurch ist
Volkstanz die feste
Einlage im Mu-
seum.

Danse folklorique,
un numéro fixe du
programme pen-
dant tout l'été.

Øverst: Kjøkkenet i Chrystie-gården.
Nederst: Sølvsmeden har verksted i «Gamlebyen».
Motstående side, øverst til venstre: Collett-gården fra Oslo.
Til høyre: Chrystie-gården fra Brevik.
Nederst: Gateparti fra «Gamlebyen».

Top: The kitchen of the Chrystie Family's mansion.
Bottom: The silversmith's workshop in the «Old Town».
Facing page, top left: The Collett mansion from Oslo.
Right: The Chrystie mansion from Brevik.
Bottom: A street in the «Old Town».

Oben: Die Küche im Chrystie-Haus.
Unten: In der «Altstadt» liegt die Werkstatt des Silberschmiedes.
Gegenüberliegende Seite, oben links: Das Collett-Haus aus Oslo.
Rechts: Das Chrystie-Haus aus Brevik.
Unten: Strassenpartie von der «Altstadt».

En haut: La cuisine de la maison Chrystie-gården.
En bas: L'orfèvre en argent a son atelier dans la «Vieille Ville».
Ci-contre, en haut et à gauche: La maison Collett-gården, d'Oslo.
A droite: La maison Chrystie-gården, de Brevik.
En bas: Prespective de rue, de la «Vieille Ville».

I «Gamlebyen» ligger en gruppe hus fra forstaden Enerhaugen. Små-kårsfolk bodde trangt i de små husene som ble bygget i midten av 1800-årene.
Motstående side, øverst: Syerskens rom i Johannes gate 12, 1890-årene.
Nederst: Snekkerverkstedet i Stupinngata 10.

The «Old Town» encompasses a cluster of houses from Enerhaugen, originally a suburb of Oslo. Pokey little dwellings, they date from the mid-19th century.
Facing page, top: The seamstress's room, Johannes gate 12, Oslo (1890s).
Bottom: Joiner's workshop in Stupinngata 10.

In der «Altstadt» liegt eine Hausgruppe von der Vorstadt Enerhaugen. Arme Leute lebten zusammengedrängt in solchen engen Wohnstätten, die Mitte des 19. Jahrhunderts gebaut wurden.
Gegenüberliegende Seite, oben: Zimmer der Näherin in Johannes-gate 12, etwa 1890.
Unten: Die Tischlerei in der Stupinn-gata 10.

Dans la «Vieille Ville» se trouve un groupe de maisons provenant du faubourg d'Enerhaugen. Les gens de condition modeste étaient petite-ment logés dans ces maisons minuscules construites au milieu du XIXème siècle.
Ci-contre, en haut: La chambre de la couturière, sise au numéro 12 de la rue Johannes, date des années 1890.
En bas: L'atelier du menuisier, 10, rue du Stupinn.

Øverst: I pottemakeriet lages bruksting med utgangspunkt i tradisjonell norsk keramikk.
Nederst: Norsk Folkemuseums restaurant — «Bygdøystuene».

Top: In the pottery are made utensils based on traditional Norwegian designs.
Bottom: The Museum restaurant, Bygdøystuene.

Oben: In der Töpferei werden Gebrauchsgegenstände nach der herkömmlichen Art des Landes hergestellt.
Unten: Das Museumsrestaurant «Bygdøystuene».

En haut: Dans l'atelier de poterie, on produit des objets ménagers dans le droit fil de la céramique traditionnelle norvégienne.
En bas: Le restaurant du Musée National Folklorique de Norvège, la «Taverne de Bygdøy».

Norsk Farmasihistorisk Museum ligger i «Gamlebyen».
Øverst: Offisinet fra apoteket «Hjorten» i Oslo, opprettet i 1857.
Nederst: Sirupskanne fra «Kong Salomons Apotek» i Fredrikstad.

The Norwegian Pharmacy Museum in the «Old Town».
Top: The dispensary of the «Hjorten» pharmacy, est. 1857.
Bottom: Syrup jug from «Kong Salomons Apotek», Fredrikstad.

Norwegisches Pharmaziehistorisches Museum liegt in der «Altstadt».
Oben: Die Offizin der Apotheke «Hjorten» in Oslo, errichtet 1857.
Unten: Sirupskanne von der Apotheke «Kong Salomon» in Fredrikstad.

Le Musée National d'Histoire de la Pharmacie se trouve dans la «Vieille Ville».
En haut: L'officine de la «Pharmacie du Cerf», d'Oslo, fondée en 1857.
En bas: Burette à sirop, provenant de la «Pharmacie du Roi Salomon», de Fredrikstad.

Øverst: Standglass fra «Løveapoteket» i Bergen, 1700-årene.
Nederst: Dansk herbarium brukt i Norge.
Motstående side: Oppsats fra Herrebøe fajansefabrikk, 1760-årene.

Top: Glass jar from «Løveapoteket», Bergen (18th century).
Bottom: Danish herbarium used in Norway.
Facing page: Cruet from Herrebøe fajansefabrikk (1760s).

Oben: Ständerglas von der «Løve-Apotheke» in Bergen, 18. Jh.
Unten: Dänisches Herbarium, in Norwegen verwendet.
Gegenüberliegende Seite: Fayence Tafelaufsatz aus Herrebøe um 1760.

En haut: Bocal, provenant de la «Pharmacie du Lion», de Bergen, et datant du XVIIIème siècle.
En bas: Herbier danois, utilisé en Norvège.
Ci-contre: Service à salade, produit à la faïencerie de Herrebø, dans les années 1760.

Bysamlingen inneholder møbler, drakter og husgeråd fra norsk bymiljø fra ca. 1550 til 1900.
Øverst: Armstol fra ca. 1710.
Nederst: Drikkekanne fra 1600-årene.
Motstående side øverst: Renessanserommet i Bysamlingen.

On display in the Urban Collection are furniture, garments and household utensils from urban Norway dating from c. 1550 to 1900.
Top: Armchair (c. 1710).
Bottom: Tankard (17th century).
Facing page, top: The Renaissance Room in the Urban Collection.

Die Stadtsammlungen umfassen Möbel, Trachten und Hausgeräte vom norwegischen Stadtmilieu in der Zeit etwa 1550 - 1900.
Oben: Armsessel, etwa 1710.
Unten: Humpen, Ende 1600.
Gegenüberliegende Seite, oben: Das Renaissance-Zimmer der Stadtsammlungen.

La Collection de la Ville renferme des meubles, des costumes et des outils ménagers de la vie urbaine de la période comprise, à peu près, entre 1550 et 1900.
En haut: Fauteuil datant de 1710 environ.
En bas: Chope datant du XVIIème siècle.
Ci-contre, en haut: Salle renaissance, de la Collection de la Ville.

Sølvsmedarbeider,
drikkekanne fra
1691, beger fra 1759
og trebolle med be-
slag fra 1500-årene.

Examples of the sil-
versmith's art — a
tankard (1691),
beaker (1759), and a
wooden bowl with
silver fittings (16th
century).

Silberschmiedarbei-
ten: Humpen 1691,
Becher 1759 und
Holznapf mit Be-
schlag vom 16. Jh.

Pièces d'argenterie,
chope datant de
1691, gobelet fait en
1759 et vase en
bois, cerclé, datant
du XVIème siècle.

Drikkehorn fra Hal-
lingdal, 1400-1500-
årene.

Drinking-horn from
Hallingdal (15-16th
century).

Trinkhorn aus Hal-
lingdal, 15.-16. Jh.

Corne à boire, pro-
venant de la Halling-
dal, et datant du
XVème ou du
XVIème siècle.

Stue fra Arendals-
katen, ca. 1760.

A drawing-room
from the Arendal
district
(c. 1760).

Kate aus der Gegend
bei Arendal, etwa
1760.

Salon provenant de
la région d'Arendal.
Env. 1760.

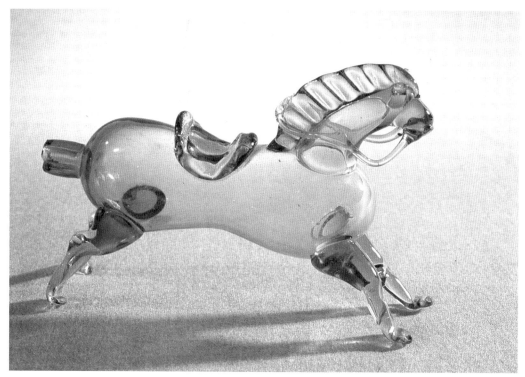

«Fyllehest» — karaffel til brennevin.

A carafe for spirits.

«Füllpferd» — Branntweinkaraffe.

«Bouteille-cheval» — carafon à eau-de-vie.

Møbelgruppe i nyrokokkostil, ca. 1850.

Neo-rococo suite (c. 1850).

Möbelgruppe im Neorokoko-Stil, etwa 1850.

Ameublement, style néo-rocaille, env. 1850.

Øverst: Dukkeskap fra 1765. Slike dukkeskap var ofte samlerobjekter for voksne.
Nederst: Trehester fra Hallingdal og Setesdal. I Leketøyutstillingen vises også en stor samling dukker.

Top: A doll cabinet (1765). Such cabinets were popular also with adults.
Bottom: Wooden horses from the Hallingdal and Setesdal valleys. The Toys section also houses a comprehensive display of dolls.

Oben: Puppenschrank aus dem Jahre 1765. Solche Puppenschränke waren oft Sammlerobjekte der Erwachsenen.
Unten: Holzpferde aus Hallingdal und Setesdal. Die Spielzeugausstellung umfasst eine erhebliche Puppensammlung.

En haut: Armoire à jouets, datant de 1765. Les armoires à jouets de ce genre étaient souvent recherchées, par les adultes, comme objets de collection.
En bas: Chevaux de bois, provenant des Hallingdal et Setesdal. L'exposition de jouets nous montre d'autre part une grande collection de poupées.

Øverst: Henrik Ibsens arbeidsværelse, ca. 1900.
Nederst: Reiseveske, vadsekk, fra 1870-årene, brodert med perler og ullgarn.

Top: The playwright Henrik Ibsen's study (c. 1900).
Bottom: Carpet-bag from the 1870s, embroidered with pearls and woollen yarn.

Oben: Arbeitszimmer Henrik Ibsens, etwa um 1900.
Unten: Reisetasche, Lodensack, etwa um 1870, gestickt mit Perlen und Wollgarn.

En haut: Cabinet de travail de Henrik Ibsen, env. 1900.
Eb bas: Trousse, sac de voyage, des années 1870, brodé de perles et de fils de laine.

Øverst: I Kirkesamlingen vises etterreformatorisk inventar fra forskjellige norske kirker. Her holdes også gudstjenester og konserter.
Nederst: Tysk klavikord fra 1747.

Top: On exhibition in the Ecclesiastical section are post-Reformation objects from a variety of Norwegian churches. Religious services and concerts are also held here.
Bottom: German clavichord (1747).

Oben: Die Kirchensammlung umfasst nachreformatorisches Mobiliar von verschiedenen norwegischen Kirchen. Hier werden auch Gottesdienste und Konzerte abgehalten.
Unten: Deutsches Klavichord aus dem Jahre 1747.

En haut: Dans la collection consacrée au culte, on voit du mobilier datant d'après la Réforme et provenant de diverses églises norvégiennes. On y célèbre d'ailleurs des offices, puis on y donne des concerts.
En bas: Clavicorde allemand, datant de 1747.·

Norsk Folkemuseum har mer enn 20.000 tekstiler og motedrakter i sine samlinger.
Side 41: Billedteppe fra Gudbrandsdalen. Teppet er trolig laget i 1700-årene og viser de fem kloke og de fem dårlige jomfruene.
Denne side, øverst: Silkekjole fra 1790-årene.
Nederst: Importert strikket silketrøye med broderi av forgylt sølvtråd, 1600-årene.
Motstående side, øverst til venstre: Bomullskjole fra ca. 1860.
Til høyre: Skidrakt fra 1890.
Nederst: Teppe i dobbeltvev fra Gudbrandsdalen.
Side 44: Teppene som er utstilt i museets teppesal har hovedsaklig vært brukt til sengetepper.
Øverst, til venstre: Ruteåkle fra Rogaland.
Til høyre: Putetrekk i halvfloss fra Gudbrandsdalen.
Nederst, til venstre: Bolster, trolig fra Møre og Romsdal.
Til høyre: Skillbragdteppe fra Vest-Agder.

The Norwegian Folk Museum possesses more than 20,000 textiles and fashions.
Page 41: Tapestry from Gudbrandsdal. Probably 18th century, it depicts the five wise and five foolish virgins.
This page, top: Silk dress (1790s).
Bottom: Imported knitted silk shirt embroidered in gilded silver thread (17th century).
Facing page, top left: Cotton dress (c. 1860).
Right: Skiing outfit (1890).
Bottom: Coverlet in pick-up double cloth, Gudbrandsdal.
Page 44: Most of the tapestries on display did duty as coverlets.
Top, left: Tapestry from Rogaland.
Right: Cushion cover in voided pile fabric, Gudbrandsdal.
Bottom, left: Ticking, probably from Møre og Romsdal.
Right: Weft-patterned tabby tapestry from Vest-Agder.

Die Sammlungen des Norwegischen Volksmuseums umfassen mehr als 20.000 Textilien und modische Trachten.
Seite 41: Bildteppich aus Gudbrandsdal. Der Teppich stammt vermutlich vom 18. Jh. und stellt die fünf klugen und die fünf schlechten Jungfrauen dar.
Diese Seite, oben: Seidenes Kleid aus den Jahren um 1790.
Unten: Importiertes Strickwams mit Stickerei aus vergoldetem Silberfaden, etwa 17. Jh.
Gegenüberliegende Seite, oben links: Kleid aus Baumwolle, etwa 1860.
Rechts: Skianzug aus den Jahren um 1890.
Unten: Teppich in Doppelgewebe, aus Gudbrandsdal.
Seite 44: Die im Teppichsaal des Museums ausgestellten Teppiche wurden hauptsächlich als Bettdecken verwendet.
Oben, links: Teppich mit Karomuster, aus Rogaland.
Rechts: Kopfkissenbezug aus halber Samenvolle, Gudbrandsdal.
Unten, links: Bettdecke, vermutlich aus Møre und Romsdal.
Rechts: Teppich mit Einschlagsmuster aus Vest-Agder.

Le Musée National Folklorique de Norvège conserve dans ses collection plus de 20.000 textiles et vêtements de modes.
Page 41: Tapisserie historiée, provenant de la Gudbrandsdal. Réalisée probablement au XVIIIème siècle, elle nous montre les cinq vierges sages et les cinq vierges folles.
La présente page, en haut: Robe en soie, datant des années 1790.
En bas: Camisole en tricot de soie, importée, brodée de fil de vermeil, datant du XVIIème siècle.
Ci-contre, en haut et à gauche: Robe en coton, 1860 env.
A droite: Habillement de skieur, datant de 1890.
En bas: Tapisserie double-face, provenant de la Gudbrandsdal.
Page 44: Les tapisseries exposées dans la salle des tissages du Musée ont avant tout servi de dessus de lit.
En haut et à gauche: Tapisserie à carreaux provenant de la province de Rogaland.
A droite: Taie d'oreiller en molletonné, provenant de la Gudbrandsdal.
En bas et à gauche: Coutil, provenant probablement de la province de Møre et Romsdal.
A droite: Tissage lancé et broché, provenant de Vest-Agder.

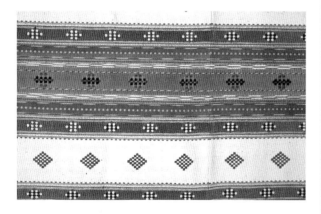

I Telemark og Setesdal var innredning og husgeråd preget av middelaldersk form og dekor til opp i 1800-årene.
Øverst: Seng med karveskurd fra Telemark.
Nederst, til venstre: Ullkurv fra Telemark i stolpekonstruksjon.
Til høyre: Øløse fra Setesdal.

Mediaeval design and decor continued to characterise furnishings and household utensils in Telemark and Setesdal until some way into the 19th century.
Top: Carved bed from Telemark.
Bottom, left: A box for wool from Telemark.
Right: Ale ladle from Setesdal.

Bis ins 19. Jahrhundert waren in Telemark und Setesdal die Einrichtungen und Hausgeräte durch mittelalterliche Formen und Dekoren geprägt.
Oben: Bett mit Kerbschnitzerei aus Telemark.
Unten, links: Wollkorb mit Pfostenkonstruktion, aus Telemark.
Rechts: Bierkelle aus Setesdal.

Formes et décor médiévaux donnent leur empreinte à l'ameublement et aux ustensiles de ménage dans le Telemark et dans la Setesdal, jusque loin dans le XIXème siècle.
En haut: Lit décoré en taille d'épargne, provenant du Telemark.
En bas et à gauche: Boîte à laine, renforcée de bâtons, provenant du Telemark.
A droite: Louche à bière, provenant de la Setesdal.

I 1700-årene begynte en blomstringsperiode i folkekunsten på Østlandet. Interiørene ble preget av nye møbeltyper og av rosemaling og treskurd med akantusmotiver.
Øverst: «Kroneseng» fra Østfold, ca. 1800.
Nederst, til venstre: Hengeskap med akantusskurd fra Gudbrandsdalen.
Til høyre: «Trøys» til øl, fra Hol i Hallingdal, 1843.

In the 18th century the folk art of eastern Norway began to blossom out. New types of furniture were introduced and household interiors were full of «rose paintings» and acanthus-style carvings.
Top: «Crown bed» from Østfold (c. 1800).
Bottom, left: Wall cupboard with acanthus carvings from Gudbrandsdal.
Right: Lipped ale bowl from Hol, Hallingdal (1843).

In den 1700-Jahren begann in Ostnorwegen eine Blütezeit in der Volkskunst. Neue Möbeltypen, sowie Dekoren mit Rosenmalerei und Schnitzarbeiten mit Akanthusmotiven prägten die Inneneinrichtungen.
Oben: «Kronenbett» aus Østfold, etwa um 1800.
Unten, links: Wandschrank mit Akanthusschnitzerei, aus Gudbrandsdal.
Rechts: Bierschüssel aus Hol in Hallingdal, 1843.

Les années 1700 marquent, dans l'art folklorique de la province d'Østlandet, le début d'un âge d'or. Les intérieurs se caractérisent dès lors par de nouveaux types de meubles, par des décorations florales peintes et par des oeuvres en taille de bois représentant des motifs d'acanthe.
En haut: Lit surmonté d'une couronne, de l'Østfold (env. 1800).
En bas et à gauche: Armoire suspendue décorée de motifs d'acanthe, en taille de bois à relief, provenant de la Gudbrandsdal.
A droite: Vase à bière provenant de Hol, dans la Hallingdal (1843).

Rosemalt tak og
seng med jaktscener
fra «uppstugu», — et
gjesterom i boligens
andre etasje, — fra
Sauherad i Telemark.

Rose-painted ceiling
and bed adorned
with hunting scenes
from an upper floor
guestroom from Sau-
herad, Telemark.

Decke mit Rosen-
malerei und Bett mit
Jagdscenen in «upp-
stugu» — einem
Gästezimmer in
ersten Stock eines
Wohnhauses, aus
Sauherad in Tele-
mark.

Plafond à décoration
florale peinte, et un lit
décoré de scènes de
chasse, provenant
de la «chambre d'en
haut» — chambre
d'amis aménagée au
premier étage —
d'une maison d'ha-
bitation de Sauhe-
rad, dans le
Telemark.

Kister var ofte «bru-
dekister» brukt til de
unge jentenes utstyr.
Fra Ål i Hallingdal,
1800.

Chests like this one
from Ål, Hallingdal
(1800), were often
used to store the
linen of aspiring
brides.

Truhen wurden oft
als «Brauttruhen» zur
Aufhebung der Aus-
rüstungen der hei-
ratsfähigen Mädchen
verwendet. Aus Ål in
Hallingdal, 1800.

Les bahuts renfer-
maient souvent les
trousseaux des futu-
res jeunes mariées.
Celle-ci, datant de
1800, provient d'Ål,
dans la Hallingdal.

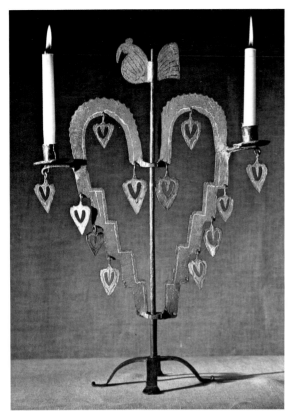

Lysestake av smijern fra Hol i Hallingdal, ca. 1800.

Wrought-iron candelabrum from Hol, Hallingdal (c. 1800).

Leuchter aus Schmiedeisen. Hol in Hallingdal, etwa um 1800.

Chandelier en fer forgé, environ 1800, et provenant de Hol, dans la Hallingdal.

Tutekanne brukt til øl ved høytider. Fra Rollag i Numedal.

Ale tankard with spout for ceremonial occasions from Rollag, Numedal.

Schnabelkanne für Bier zum Festgebrauch. Aus Rollag in Numedal.

Pot à bière, avec goulot, réservé aux grandes occasions. Provenant de Rollag, dans la Numedal.

Grøtspann, «ambar», ble brukt til rømmegrøten på festbordet. Fra Gudbrandsdalen.

A pail for «rømmegrøt» (sour-cream porridge) from Gudbrandsdal.

Holzgefäss für «Sauerrahmbrei», für den Festtisch vorgesehen. Aus Gudbrandsdal.

Seillette à couvercle, pour la bouille à la crème fraiche destinée au banquet. Provenant de la Gudbrandsdal.

Øverst: Dette maleriet fra 1699 av storbonden Bjørn Frøysaak og hans familie viser lokal draktskikk i Hallingdal, sterkt preget av renessansens bymote.
Nederst: Skrin med karveskurd fra Vossestrand i Hordaland.

Top: This painting from 1699 of a prosperous farmer, Bjørn Frøysaak, and his family affords an insight into contemporary Hallingdal fashions, which were strongly influenced by urban renaissance styles.
Bottom: Carved casket from Vossestrand, Hordaland.

Oben: Gemälde aus dem Jahre 1699 von dem Grossbauer Bjørn Frøysaak und seiner Familie zeigt den örtlichen Trachtengebrauch in Hallingdal, der durch die städtischen Moden der Renaissance stark beeinflusst war.
Unten: Schrein mit Kerbschnitzarbeiten, aus Vossestrand in Hordaland.

En haut. Cette peinture, datant de 1699 et reproduisant Bjørn Frøysaak, paysan cossu, et sa famille, nous documente sur les traditions vestimentaires locales de la Hallingdal, en l'occurrence fortement influencées par la mode citadine de la Renaissance.
En bas: Ecrin décoré en taille d'épargne, provenant de Vossestrand, dans la province de Hordaland.

Melkebøtte, stavkinne til smør og melkeringe med sil liggende over. Fedrift var en viktig del av landbruket. De vanligste husdyra var ku, sau og geit, som alle ble melket.

Milk pail, butter churn and curd bowl with strainer. Cattle-raising was a mainstay of Norwegian farming. The commonest domestic animals were cows, sheep and goats, all of which were milked.

Milcheimer, Butterfass mit Stössel, und Fass mit Sieb für Setzmilch. Viehzucht war ein wichtiger Teil der Landwirtschaft. Die üblichen Haustiere waren Kühe, Schafe und Ziegen, die alle gemolken wurden.

Seille à lait, baratte à piston pour faire le beurre, et vase à lait avec passoire. L'élévage du bétail constituait une partie importante de l'agriculture. Les animaux les plus habituels: vaches, brebis et chèvres, étaient, tous, exploités pour le lait.

Øverst: Oppstadveven med tøybom oppe og «kljåsteiner» nede som strammer renningen, er kjent fra forhistorisk tid. Den hadde stor utbredelse, men er i vår tid bare kjent i bruk i Norge.

Nederst: Rokk, snellestol og ulike typer garnvinder fra utstillingen av tekstilredskaper.

Top: The principle of the vertical loom with a clothbeam at the top and a weight at the bottom to tauten the warp was known in prehistoric times. Its use was once widespread, but nowadays Norway is the only place where it is known to be still employed.

Bottom: Spinning-wheel, bobbin holder and yarn reels from the Textiles section.

Oben: Oppstadveven mit Tuchbaum oben und Steingewichten («kljåsteiner») unten zum Straffen der Kette, ist von vorgeschichtlicher Zeit bekannt. Dieser Webstuhl war einmal weit verbreitet, ist aber heute vermutlich nur in Norwegen in Gebrauch.

Unten: Spinnrad, Rollengestell ungleiche Typen Garnwinden, aus der Ausstellung der Textilgeräte.

En haut: Déchargeoir en haut, et de pierres étireuses pour serrer la lice en bas, Oppstadveven est d'un type qui nous est connu dès l'aube de l'histoire. D'emploi tout à fait général autrefois, il ne semble plus, de nos jours, être en usage ailleurs qu'en Norvège.

En bas: Rouet, support de bobines et différents types de dévidoirs; de l'exposition de l'outillage des textiles et du tissage.

Museet har en egen billedsamling.

Øverst: Setesdøl med kløvhest. Kløvjing var en vanlig transportmåte, og egnet seg godt på eldre tiders dårlige veier.

I midten: Høyet ble slått med ljå, raket sammen og hengt på hesjer for å tørke. Deretter ble det båret i hus eller kjørt inn på slede.

Nederst: Ard av tre med jernbeslag. Arden er det eldste pløyeredskapet, brukt i Norden allerede i bronsealderen. I enkelte deler av Norge har den vært brukt fram til vår tid.

Motstående side, øverst: Høvre fra Gudbrandsdalen. Hestens seletøy var ofte rikt dekorert.

Nederst, til venstre: Kløvsal og åkle, — slitte åklær ble gjerne brukt til hestedekken.

Til høyre: Når buskapen var ute på beite hang man bjeller på lederdyret i flokken. Bjelleklaven hadde vakkert mønster.

The Museum also boasts a picture archive.

Top: A man from Setesdal with packhorse. Horses were a common mode of transport and well suited to the poor roads of old.

Centre: Hay was cut with a scythe, raked into heaps and hung on racks to dry. It was subsequently carried into barns on the farmworkers' backs or dragged in on sledges.

Bottom: Wooden plough with iron-shod share. This type of plough is the world's oldest and was in use in the North as far back as the Bronze Age. In some parts of Norway its use persisted right down to modern times.

Facing page, top: Hame from Gudbrandsdal. Harness was often lavishly decorated.

Bottom, left: Packhorse saddle and coverlet. Worn coverlets tended to end up as horse blankets.

Right: When animals were put out to pasture a bell suspended from a richly ornamented collar was hung on the leader.

Das Museum hat eine eigene Bildersammlung.

Oben: Mann aus Setesdal mit Saumpferd. Befördern mit Saumpferd war die übliche Transportweise, die sich auf den damaligen schlechten Wegen gut eignete.

Mitte: Das Heu wurde mit Sense gemäht, zusammengerecht und zum Trocknen auf «Norwegenreuter» aufgehängt. Anschliessend wurde es auf dem Rücken oder mit einem Schlitten in die Scheune gebracht.

Unten: Holzpflug mit eisenbeschlagener Schar. Zum Pflügen ist der Holzpflug das älteste Gerät, das bereits in der Bronzzeit im Norden verwendet wurde. In einzelnen Bezirken in Norwegen waren Holzpflüge bis auf unsere Tage im Gebrauch.

Gegenüberliegende Seite, oben: Kumt aus Gudbrandsdal. Die Geschirre waren oft reichlich dekoriert.

Unten, links: Saumsattel und Teppich. Ausgetragene Teppiche wurden oft als Pferdedecken verwendet.

Rechts: Die Leittiere der weidenden Herden trugen Schellen. Die Schellenjoche waren in der Regel schön verziert.

Le Musée a sa propre collection iconographique.

En haut: Habitant de la Setesdal, tenant un cheval de bât. D'emploi courant, le transport à dos de bêtes de somme était ce qu'il y avait de plus adapté aux mauvaises routes d'autrefois.

A milieu: Ayant fauché l'herbe, on la ramassait à l'aide de rateaux, puis la disposait sur des séchoirs. On ramenait ensuite le foin à la grange, soit en le prenant sur le dos, soit en le chargeant sur des traîneaux.

En bas: Araire en bois, à lame revêtue de fer. L'araire, le plus vieil instrument de labour qu'on connaisse, était employé en Scandinavie déjà à l'âge du bronze. Dans certaines régions de la Norvège, il a été utilisé jusqu'à un date très proche de notre propre époque.

Ci-contre, en haut: Pièce dorsale d'un harnais d'attelage, provenant de la Gudbrandsdal. Le harnais des chevaux était souvent richement décoré.

En bas et à gauche: Bât et tapisserie, — les tapisseries usées servaient souvent de couverture de cheval.

A droite: Amenant le bétail en pâturage, on attachait une cloche à l'animal de tête du troupeau. Le collier avait une belle ornementation.

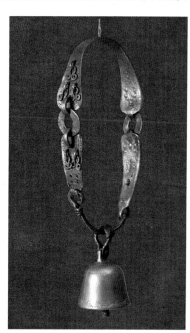

Øverst til venstre: «Beltekluter» brukt av bruden. Fra Bø i Telemark.
Til høyre: Kvinneskjorte fra Øst-Telemark.
Nederst: Forkle av ulldamask fra Lunde i Telemark.
Motstående side, øverst: Brudekrone fra Hardanger.
Nederst: Linforkle med Hardangersøm.

Top, left: A bride's aprons from Bø, Telemark.
Right: Woman's shirt from eastern Telemark.
Bottom: Apron of woollen damask from Lunde, Telemark.
Facing page, top: Bridal crown from Hardanger.
Bottom: Hardanger-embroidered linen apron.

Oben links: «Beltschürzen», von der Braut getragen. Aus Bø in Telemark.
Rechts: Frauenhemd aus Ost-Telemark.
Unten: Schürze aus Wolldamast, aus Lunde in Telemark.
Gegenüberliegende Seite, oben: Brautkrone aus Hardanger.
Unten: Schürze aus Leinentuch mit Hardanger-Stickerei.

En haut et à gauche: Napperons de ceinture, pour la jeune mariée. Provenant de Bø, dans le Telemark.
A droite: Camisole de femme, du Telemark oriental.
En bas: Tablier en damas de laine, provenant de Lunde, dans le Telemark.
Ci-contre, en haut: Couronne de jeune mariée, provenant de Hardanger.
En bas: Tablier, à bordure brodée dans le style de Hardanger.

Øverst: Mannsvest fra Valle i Setesdal.
Nederst: Brudgommens pyntelommetørkle. Fra Hardanger.
Motstående side, øverst: Kvinnekåpe av ulldamask fra Sigdal.
Nederst: Detalj av forklebord fra Telemark.

Top: Man's waistcoat from Valle, Setesdal.
Bottom: Bridegroom's dress handkerchief from Hardanger.
Facing page, top: Woman's cape in woollen damask from Sigdal.
Bottom: Detail of apron trimming from Telemark.

Oben: Männerweste aus Valle in Setesdal.
Unten: Taschentuch des Bräutigams. Aus Hardanger.
Gegenüberliegende Seite, oben: Frauenumhang aus Wolldamast, Sigdal.
Unten: Detail einer Schürzenborte, aus Telemark.

En haut: Gilet d'homme, de Valle, dans la Setesdal.
En bas: Mouchoir du marié, de Hardanger.
Ci-contre, en haut: Pèlerine en damas de laine broché, provenant de Sigdal.
En bas: Détail de la bordure d'un tablier, provenant du Telemark.

57

Norsk Folkemuseum har en av verdens største samlinger av samisk folkekunst. Eksemplene på de følgende sidene avspeiler noe av det kulturelle mangfoldet innenfor denne folkegruppen, som bor spredt over et vidstrakt område i fire land.

The Norwegian Folk Museum has one of the world's largest collections of Lapp folk art. The specimens pictured in the following pages reflect the cultural range of this ethnic group, who live widely dispersed over a vast territory encompassing parts of four countries.

Das Ausstellungsgut lappischer Volkskunst im Besitze des Norwegischen Volksmuseums umfasst eine der grössten Sammlungen der Welt. An den folgenden Seiten spiegeln die Abbildungen nur einen Teil des kulturellen Vielfalts dieser Volksgruppe ab. Die Lappen leben verstreut in einem weitausgedehnten Gebiet, das sich über vier Länder erstreckt.

Le Musée National Folklorique de Norvège possède une des plus grandes collections du monde d'art lapon. Les échantillons reproduits dans les pages suivantes reflètent quelque peu la diversité culturelle de ce groupe ethnique qui, clairsemé, occupe de vastes régions s'étendant sur quatre pays.

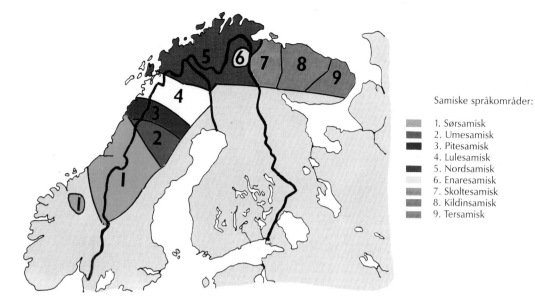

Samiske språkområder:

1. Sørsamisk
2. Umesamisk
3. Pitesamisk
4. Lulesamisk
5. Nordsamisk
6. Enaresamisk
7. Skoltesamisk
8. Kildinsamisk
9. Tersamisk

Die lappischen Sprachgebiete umfassen:

1. Südlappisch
2. Umelappisch
3. Pitelappisch
4. Lulelappisch
5. Nordlappisch
6. Enarelappisch
7. Skoltelappisch
8. Kildinlappisch
9. Terlappisch

Voici la carte linguistique lapponne:

1. Branche méridionale
2. Branche uméoise
3. Branche pitéoise
4. Branche luléoise
5. Branche septentrionale
6. Branche énaréoise
7. Branche scoltéoise
8. Branche kildinnoise
9. Branche terroise

Lapp language areas:

1. South-Lappish
2. Ume-Lappish
3. Pite-Lappish
4. Lule-Lappish
5. North-Lappish
6. Enare-Lappish
7. Skolte-Lappish
8. Kildin-Lappish
9. Ter-Lappish

Samiske drakter fra venstre: Skoltesamisk (fra grenseområdet mellom Norge, Finland og Sovjet Unionen), sørsamisk (Røros), nordsamiske og lulesamiske (Tysfjord).

Lapp costumes l to r: Skolte (from the frontier zone where Norway, Finland and the URSS conjoin), south (Røros), north and Lule, (Tysfjord).

Lappische Trachten von links nach rechts: Skolte (vom Grenzgebiet, wo Norwegen, Finnland und Rußland zusammentreffen), Süden (Røros) nordlappisch und Lule (Tysfjord).

Costumes lapons, de gauche à droite: Skolte (de la zone de frontière, là où la Norvège, la Finlande et l'Union Soviétique se touchent), le Sud (Røros) le Nord et Lule (Tysfjord).

Øverst til venstre: Hos sørsamene blir drakten dekorert med broderier av tinntråd eller perler.
Til høyre: Glassperler er brukt også på den lulesamiske pungen.
Nederst: Vevde bånd og belter med fargeglade mønstre er typisk for nordsamisk draktskikk.

Top, left: South - Lapps decorated their costumes with tin-thread embroidery or pearls.
Right: A Lule-Lapp purse, also embellished with glass pearls.
Bottom: Woven bands and belts in colourful patterns, typical of North-Lapp garments.

Oben links: Die Trachten der Südlappen werden mit Zinndrähten oder Perlen gesäumt.
Rechts: Lulelappischer Beutel mit Glasperlendekor.
Unten: Gewebte Bänder und Gürtel mit farbfreudigen Mustern, die beim nordlappischen Trachtengebrauch typisch sind.

Les Lapons de la branche méridionale décorent leurs costumes de verroteries ou de broderies au fils d'étain.
A droite: Des perles en verroterie ont également été utilisées pour la bourse à droite, provenant des régions luléoises.
En bas: Des ceintures et des rubans tissés, décorés de ces motifs hauts en couleur qui sont caractéristiques des traditions vestimentaires des Lapons de la branche septentrionale.

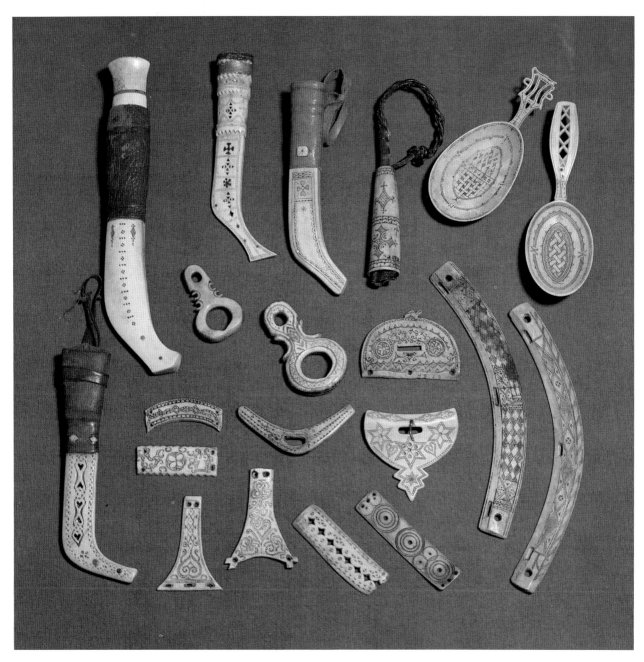

Ingen steder kommer rikdommen i samisk folkekunst bedre til uttrykk enn i bein- og hornsløyden. Bildet viser kniver, beltebeslag, nålehus, lassoringer m.m. fra ulike områder. Dekoren varierer fra geometrisk flettverk i sør til rosetter i nord.

Nowhere is the richness of Lapp folk art more in evidence than in their mastery of bone and horn carving. Seen here are knives, belt fittings, needlecases, lassoo rings and other objects from different localities. The decor ranges from geometrical tracery in the south to rosettes in the north.

Nirgends kommt der Reichtum der lappischen Volkskunst besser zum Ausdruck als bei den Bein- oder Hornwerken. Die Abbildung zeigt Messer, Gürtelbeschläge, Nadelbehälter, Lassoringe u. ä. der verschiedenen Gebiete. Der Dekor variiert von geometrischem Flechtwerk im Süden bis Rosetten im Norden.

Nulle part la richesse de l'art folklorique lapon ne s'impose avec plus d'évidence que dans les travaux en os ou en corne. Ces reproductions nous montrent des couteaux, des plaques de ceinture, des aiguillers, des boucles de lasso, etc., de provenance diverse. Leurs décorations varient, depuis des entrelacs géométriques dans les zones meridionales jusqu'à des rosettes dans le Nord.

Øverst til venstre: Tegerarbeider — dåse, flaske og osteform.
Til høyre: Drikkekopp og melkebolle.
I midten: Pulk.
Nederst: Bunnen av en runebomme — en magisk tromme — fra Hamarøy i Nordland. Kjedene av tinntråd har hørt til en lignende tromme, og stammer fra Namdalen.

Top, left: Basketry - a casket, drinking vessel, and cheese mould.
Right: Drinking cup and milk bowl.
Centre: A reindeer sleigh («pulk»).
Bottom: The base of a «runebomme», a magic drum, from Hamarøy, Nordland. The tin-wire chains derive from a similar drum from Namdal.

Oben, links: Korgarbeiten — Dose, Flasche und Käseform.
Rechts: Trinknapf und Milchschüssel.
Mitte: Pulk.
Unten: Der Boden einer Zaubertrommel aus Hamarøy, Nordland. Die Zinndrahtketten gehörten ursprünglich einer ähnlichen Trommel und stammen aus Namdalen.

En haut et à gauche: Objets d'arts ménagers: Une boîte, une bouteille et un moule pour le fromage.
A droite: Un gobelet et un vase pour le lait.
Au milieu: Un traîneau d'attelage de renne.
En bas: Le fond d'un tambour runique (de force magique ...), provenant de Hamarøy, dans la province de Nordland. Les chaînettes en fil d'étain, provenant de Namdalen, ont appartenu à un tambour semblable.

Øverst: Av de 30.000 samene i Norge er det ca. 700 familier som lever av reindrift. Fjell-samene i Finnmark flytter med reinflokkene mellom sommerbeiter ved kysten og vinter-beiter i innlandet.
Nederst: Teltet er fremdeles en praktisk bolig, mens den tradisjonelle pulken er avløst av snøscooter.

Top: Of the 30,000 Lapps resident in Norway, some 700 families depend for their liveli-hood on reindeer breeding. The mountain Lapps of Finnmark migrate with their herds between summer pastures on the coast and winter pastures inland.
Bottom: Practical as they are, tents are still in common use, but the sledge has given way to the snow scooter.

Oben: Unter den etwa 30.000 Lappen in Norwegen leben etwa 700 Familien von Rennti-erwirtschaft. Die Gebirgslappen in Finnmark ziehen mit ihren Renntierherden zwischen die Sommerweiden an der Küste und die Winterweiden im Inland.
Unten: Das Zelt ist noch immer eine praktische Wohnung, der traditionelle Pulk wurde jedoch vom Motorschlitten abgelöst.

En haut: Parmi les quelque 30.000 Lapons norvégiens, on compte environ 700 familles vivant de l'exploitation de leurs rennes. Les Lapons montagnards du Finmark errent avec leurs troupeaux, passant tour à tour des pâturages estivaux près de la côte, à ceux de l'hi-ver, dans l'arrière-pays, et vice-versa.
En bas: Si la tente est encore une habitation pratique, l'attelage de renne, lui, a été rem-placé par le scooter de neige.

Tekst: Museets konservatorer og undervisningsavdeling.

Text by the curators and Educational Department of the Museum.

Text: Kustoden und Mitarbeiter der Unterrichtsabteilung des Museums.

Textes établis par les membres de la Conservation et du Service éducatif du Museé.

Omslagets bakside: Dørparti, Tveitoloftet fra Telemark, ca. 1300.

Rear cover: Door of a Telemark storehouse, Tveitoloftet (c. 1300).

Rückseite: Türpartie, Vorratshaus Tveito, Telemark, etwa 1300.

Sur la couverture, derrière: L'entrée de la maisonnette à étage de Tveito, dans le Telemark (env. 1300).